YOUR KNOWLEDGE HAS VALUE

Magdalena Zettl

Has there been a power shift from states to non-governmental organizations in world politics?

GRIN Verlag

Bibliografische Information der Deutschen Nationalbibliothek:

Die Deutsche Bibliothek verzeichnet diese Publikation in der Deutschen National-
bibliografie; detaillierte bibliografische Daten sind im Internet über http://dnb.d-
nb.de/ abrufbar.

Imprint:

Copyright © 2013 GRIN Verlag GmbH
Druck und Bindung: Books on Demand GmbH, Norderstedt Germany
ISBN: 978-3-656-53586-7

This book at GRIN:

http://www.grin.com/en/e-book/264166/has-there-been-a-power-shift-from-states-
to-non-governmental-organizations

Has there been a power shift from states to non-governmental organizations in world politics?

In the traditional IR theory of realism, states are regarded as the principal, unitary actors within the international system. While anarchy is underlying the international system, states' main concern is survival and security over other states. As no higher authority exists, states are the ones who hold control and power. Since the end of the Cold War, however, this view of states has been questioned. State power has declined and has been reallocated "among states, markets and civil society" (Mathews, 1997: 50). Among non-state actors, i.e. international organizations, such as the World Bank, non-governmental organizations (NGO), such as Amnesty International, and multi-national companies, such as Shell, especially NGOs have taken on a more influential role in world politics. NGOs have increased in quantity, from 14,000 in 1985 to about 40,000 in 2013 (APA, 2013); they have expanded in their functional areas, from advocates to service providers and mobilizers of civil society groups and have developed from small, rather unimportant organizations to equal partners for governments.

In IR, there are two main views on this phenomenon: some scholars (Lipschutz, 1992; Mathews, 1997; Keck & Sikkink, 1998; Rosenau, 2002) see the emergence of NGOs from a bottom-up perspective and argue that the decline in state power is a causal consequence of the increasing emergence of non-state actors in a zero-sum-relationship. Others (Reimann 2006, Sending & Neumann, 2006) view NGO growth as a top-down process and assert that states encourage NGO development and that non-state actors and nation-states merge into one network not sharing a limited amount of power but expanding on power.

After providing a definition of the term *power* and an understanding of NGOs, this essay lays out sound arguments rejecting the view presented in Mathews (1997) but agreeing with Reimann (2006), Sending & Neumann (2006). This essay argues for a cooperative, complementing relationship between states and NGOs instead of a hierarchical relationship in a zero-sum power game.

According to the definition of ECOSOC[1], NGOs refer to "any group of people relating to each other regularly in some formal manner and engaging in collection actions". NGOs' activities entail the following characteristics: "non-commercial, non-violent, (...) not on behalf of a government" (Willetts, 2002). According to Willetts (2002), NGOs often deviate from this definition in practice as some are connected with political parties or rely on financial resources from commercial activities. Nevertheless, NGOs have emerged as influential players in world politics from the 1970s onwards, mainly due to the UN Article 71[2] and the active inclusion of NGOs in UN conferences. This

---

[1] ECOSOC refers to the United Nations Economic and Social Council.
[2] Article 71 has given NGOs major "political opportunities such as formal international recognition and accreditation for participating in UN international conferences" (Reimann, 2006: 50).

culminated in a "new pro-NGO norm" (Reimann, 2006: 59) in the 1980s and 1990s, including major funding from states and foundations (Reimann, 2006).

Power was traditionally defined in terms of sovereignty and mainly associated with institutions of political authority. Theories focused on the type of power actors exercised instead of the actual actions. According to Foucault ([1982] 2000), however, power manifests itself in actions. Governmentality, Foucault's concept of power, refers to government as a form of power while sovereignty and discipline still remain important. Strategies and tactics play an increasingly important role in exercising power rather than institutions. Additional to Foucault's governmentality, Dean's (1999) concept of "technologies of agency" and Burchell's re-evaluation of civil society from passive to active participants of government provide a different perspective on the emergence of NGOs as influential players in world politics (Sending & Neumann, 2006).

As aforementioned, Mathews (1997) regards the power relations between states and NGOs as a zero-sum game, in which NGOs gain an increasingly influential role at the expense of state power. Taking Foucault's view on power and governmentality as presented in Sending & Neumann (2006) into account, Mathews (1997) proves to be mistaken. The state, as the provider of the welfare of the people, takes a paternal role and regards NGOs as a helping hand. In this context, the growth of non-state-actors emerges as "an expression of a change in governmentality" (Sending & Neumann, 2006: 658). Authority does no longer lie only within the state but individuals become objects as well as subjects of government. Furthermore, civil society groups, which encourage political will-formation, are an integral and central part of governing and thinking. Hence, the power, which NGOs have gained, turns out to be to the advantage and not at the expense of the state.

In general, scholars agree that the decline of state power is an effect of globalization, i.e. the rapid development of communications and transport technology as well as the inseparable economic interdependence among states and non-state actors. According to neo-liberal institutionalism, cooperation with other states and international organizations become the main vehicles in world politics to solve the emerging international problems. Hence, power does not shift necessarily to NGOs but rather to international organizations. Since these organizations, such as the European Union, are built up by the nation-states themselves, power does not completely shift away from state's hands (Jones, 2008). Furthermore, international problems request international solutions. These cannot be provided by nation-states due to their limited capacities to the national level but by actors or organizations of global scope. Hence, states consciously ask for the help of non-state actors, such as NGOs. This approves Reimann's (2006) and Sending & Neumann's (2006) top-up explanation of NGO growth and rejects Mathews's (1997) bottom-up emergence of NGOs.

While Mathews's (1997) example on the 1992 Earth Summit is well selected to prove a power shift from state to NGOs, the paper fails to analyze that NGOs take on actions, which lie outside state capacity. For example, NGOs operating worldwide are not limited to the national level but can easily tackle global problems due to their international set up. At the same time, NGOs acting locally may be better aware of local needs and can better react according to community dynamics than governments, who view problems from a national perspective. Furthermore, NGOs are not accountable to a wide population, as governments are. Also, NGOs are often specialized in a certain area, such as environment or hunger, while governments often only possess general knowledge. This allows NGOs to act and react faster and more efficiently than governments. Thereby, NGOs exert power by actions, which cannot be employed by the state.

Moreover, the relationship between states and NGOs is not one of opponents, as Mathews (1997) describes in her paper, but rather a cooperation in which the capacity of NGOs complement the capacity of the state. On the one hand, NGOs work as advocates, service providers and partners to governments. NGOs support the state in its decisions with their legal, scientific and technical expertise. Furthermore, NGOs are active on a micro-level of governance, since they mobilize civil society groups. Thereby NGOs not only make use of but also strengthen the democratic system. On the other hand, it is states that mostly sponsor NGOs (e.g. through bilateral agencies) and set the legal and fiscal requirements for the emergence and exercise of influence of NGOs. Hence, according to Reimann (2006), the nation-state and NGOs live a symbiotic relationship. Similarly, Slaughter (2004) proposes that the state and NGOs form a "New World Order" of networks in which they cooperate in specific issues areas.

To conclude, although NGOs become increasingly influential in world politics, it is, nevertheless, the state's decisions, which opportunities are given, which limits are set to NGOs and to which extent NGOs are integrated into political decisions. States remain to be the principal actors in the international system and maintain their strategic, irreplaceable role in world politics. Nevertheless, as Anne-Marie Slaughter suggests in *New World Order* (2004), nation-states and NGOs will establish networks to facilitate cooperation. Thus, scholars should not be concerned about the decline and shift of state power in world politics. Instead, as tactics and strategies become more important in the studies of global governance, scholars should examine how NGOs and more generally non-state actors can build up powerful networks with states and how NGOs can cooperate more efficiently with states, businesses and international organizations to achieve national and international goals and find solutions for global problems.

References

Anderson, K. & Rieff, D. 2005. Global Civil Society: A Sceptical View. In: H. Anheier, M. Glasius & M. Kaldor (eds.). *Global Civil Society 2004/5*. London: SAGE, 2005, pp.26-39.

APA, 2013. *NGOs, the UN and APA*. Viewed on 3rd January 2013. Accessed at < http://www.apa.org/international/united-nations/publications.aspx>.

Burchell, G. 1996 Liberal Government and Techniques of the Self. In: A. Barry, T. Osborne & N. Rose. *Foucault and Political Reason*. London: University College London.

Dean, M. 1999. *Governmentality. Power and Rule in Modern Society*. London: Sage.

Foucault, M. ([1982] 2000). The Subject and Power. In J. D. Faubion. *Power: Essential Works of Foucault 1954-1984*, Vol. 3. London: Penguin.

Jones, A. 2008. *NGOs and the Retreat of the State*. Viewed on 2nd January 2013. Accessed at < http://www.e-ir.info/2008/02/29/ngos-and-the-retreat-of-the-state/>.

Keck, M. E. & Sikkink, K. 1998. Activists Beyond Borders. *Advocacy Networks in International Politics*. Ithaca: Cornell University Press.

Lipschutz, R. D. 1992. Reconstructing World Politics: The Emergence of Global Civil Society. *Millenium: Journal of International Studies* 21:389-420.

Mathews, J. T. 1997. Power shift. *Foreign Affairs*, 76 (1): 50-66.

Reimann, K. D. 2006. A view from the top: international politics, norms and the worldwide growth of NGOs. *International Studies Quarterly*, 50 (1): 45-67.

Rosenau, J. T. & Czempiel, E.-O, eds. 1992. *Governance Without Government: Order and Change in World Politics*. Cambridge: Cambridge University Press.

Rosenau, J. T. 2002. Governance in a New Global Order. In D. Held & A. McGrew. *Governing Globalization: Power, Authority and Global Governance*. Cambridge: Polity Press.

Sending, O. & Neumann, I. 2006. Governance to Governmentality: Analyzing NGOs, States, and Power. *International Studies Quarterly*, 50(3): 651-672.

Slaughter, A. M. 2004. *A New World Order*. New Jersey: Princeton University Press.

Van Creveld, M. 2000. The State: Its Rise and Decline. *Mises Daily*. Viewed on 2nd January 2013. Accessed at <http://mises.org/daily/527>.

Willetts, P. 2002. *What is a Non-Governmental Organization?* Viewed on 3rd January 2013. Accessed at < http://www.staff.city.ac.uk/p.willetts/CS-NTWKS/NGO-ART.HTM#Start>.